CW00411169

PET OWNER'S GUIDE TO THE
ROUGH COLLIE

Stella Clark

RINGPRESS

ACKNOWLEDGEMENTS

I would like to thank Dave Baker and Enid Binns, of the
Rough and Smooth Collie Training Association, for showing even
more aspects to the Collie's versatility.
Thanks are also due to Pauline Skyrme, for assisting me with the
photographic sessions for Rough Collie care and grooming.
Finally, thanks to Marilyn, for the endless cups of coffee.

ABOUT THE AUTHOR

Stella Clark has been breeding and exhibiting Rough and Smooth
Collies since 1968. She has produced 15 UK and International
Champions to date, as well as one World Champion.
Also a Championship show judge, Stella judges five different breeds
of dog within the Pastoral Group, and has had the honour of judging
Crufts in 1993. In recent years, her knowledge of dogs has taken her
all over the world, including sitting on the judging panel for two
World Shows in Finland and Budapest.

Design: Sara Howell

**Published by Ringpress Books Limited,
PO Box 8, Lydney, Gloucestershire,
GL15 4YN, United Kingdom.**

First published 2001
©2001 Ringpress Books Limited. All rights reserved

ISBN 1 86054 198 4

Printed and bound in Hong Kong through Printworks International Ltd.

CONTENTS

SHOWING YOUR ROUGH COLLIE   48

5

A guide to the Breed Standards;
Making a Champion.

BREEDING FROM YOUR COLLIE   58

6

The stud dog; The brood bitch;
Preparations; The mating; The
pregnant bitch; Arrangements for
whelping; The big day; Second
Stage; After the birth; The nursing
mother; Weaning.

THE ROUGH COLLIE'S HEALTH   68

7

The medicine chest; Administering medicine, Treating minor
ailments; When to call your vet; What is an emergency?
(Bloat, Eye injury, Poisoning, Dog fights); Anal glands;
Artificial respiration; Asthma; Bad breath; Blindness; Burns;
Collie Nose; Constipation; Diarrhoea; Enteritis; Loss of
hair; The female
cycle; Pyometra;
False pregnancy;
Mastitis; The male
Collie; Castration;
Hereditary
diseases; Parasites;
Homoeopathic
medicine.

1 Introducing The Rough Collie

If you are reading this book, you will either be thinking of purchasing a Rough Collie, or have just done so. The choice you have made will bring you and your family so much pleasure, as the Rough Collie is a true family dog.

My first Rough Collie was bought for my son in 1968 and we have had these dogs ever since. Actually, I could never imagine life without having several Rough Collies around the home.

THE PERFECT ROUGH COLLIE

The Rough Collie is, without doubt, one of the most glamorous dogs in the world. With his truly elegant, regal bearing, he stands aloof from other breeds. He is adaptable to all lifestyles, whether they be town or country. He does not need constant attention. Given a walk twice daily, if possible, or a good free run, and a comfortable

The Rough Collie is a great family dog, particularly with children.

sleeping area, a Rough Collie will be happy with his lot.

He will join you in all aspects of your life. One of our Collies loved to come water-skiing with us and would sit in the speedboat enjoying the wind and spray on his fur. Most Rough Collies love a game of football, or just joining in any family sports. They like going for a walk but will not mind too much if this does not happen. They are just as happy lazing around.

The Rough Collie should be a sweet-natured, obedient animal, with a happy disposition. His main aim in life is to please his owner. This makes him a perfect family dog. Where a Rough Collie comes into his own is with children. He adores them and he will be a most devoted and loyal companion. He will guard without being aggressive, he will be easy to train and, above all, he will be a clean and respectful keeper of your home. Most Rough Collies live in the house and it is very rare indeed that you will find them to be destructive.

HUMAN CONTACT

Rough Collies thrive on human contact and, although they will live quite happily in a kennel, they would much prefer to be included in the family way of life. Also, my

The Smooth Collie (right) has an enthusiastic following, but it has never been as popular as the Rough Collie.

The Rough Collie still retains some of his working sheepdog instincts.

way of thinking is that, when you own such a magnificent animal as a Rough Collie, you will wish to gaze on his beauty and not hide him away in a kennel. One look from those beautiful eyes and you will be hooked. As the Rough Collie is such a clean dog, you will love to see him about the home.

You will all have heard of Lassie, the famous Collie film star, and I am sure, like me, you have wept many a tear over these films. In 1940 Eric Knight wrote the classic book *Lassie Come Home*, and when Metro Goldwyn Mayer decided to make a film of the book, Lassie became the idol of dog lovers worldwide. It is interesting to note that six films were made, all of them leaving Collie lovers enthralled, watching this magnificent dog saving people's lives by snatching them from burning houses, and swollen rivers. Lassie was every youngster's dream. The last Lassie film was made in 1951, much to the disappointment of the thousands of fans.

However, in 1954 a series of Lassie films were made for television and a total of 589 episodes were shown throughout the world, so another generation of Collie lovers came into being and boosted the popularity of the Rough Collie again.

EARLY SHEPHERD DOGS

For as long as there have been flocks of sheep and herds of cattle, there has always been a type of shepherd dog. When the Romans

The Rough Collie and the Shetland Sheepdog (front) share a similarity of type.

invaded Britain, they brought with them sheep and cattle to feed their armies and they also brought dogs to protect this livestock. In all probability, the Collie is a direct descendent from these ancient shepherding dogs.

We do know that the Collie is one of Britain's oldest breeds, dating back centuries. In early books written on shepherd breeds the word Collie, used to describe these dogs, has been spelt in many ways. The word Coll, or Colley, described black dogs. In Anglo-Saxon times the word Col meant black, and the shepherd-type dogs were called after the black-faced sheep common at that time. As, up until at least 1871, these dogs were black, or black and tan, we would assume, although there is no direct evidence, that the Rough Collie of today is a direct descendant.

THE EVOLUTION OF THE BREED

For the Rough Collie's early development, we should look to the north of England where a dog was needed to assist the shepherd in some of the worst weather conditions. Those dogs were slightly smaller and stockier in build than the Rough Collie we see today, but they became very popular as they were easy to train and proved to be most loyal. They were so intelligent and eager to please that it was not long before hill farmers started to take them to assist them in their work, and it seems that a good working Collie quite often changed hands for vast sums of money.

It was during the early 1800s that many changes took place in the breeding of the Rough Collie, resulting in the dog we see today, and through selective breeding the Border Collie-type head became more refined, with a flatter skull and longer muzzle.

When it became known that Queen Victoria had seen Rough Coated Collies working on her estates, and had been so impressed that she brought several back to her kennels, word soon got round and the Americans then became infatuated with this glamorous new breed.

The Rough Collie took America by storm. Dog breeders were overwhelmed by this long-coated, intelligent dog, and because of this, the Rough Collie was in great demand, with many being shipped out to the USA at prices much higher than those paid even today, such was the popularity of this new, emerging breed.

Many Rough Collies left England in those early days of development, going to large breeding establishments in America where they became, and still are, one of America's most popular dogs.

From its humble beginnings as a farm dog, the Rough Collie had now become a much sought-after companion. Queen Victoria had a favourite as one of her constant companions and this made the Rough Collie one of the most coveted dogs of the day.

THE ROUGH COLLIE TODAY

The first Breed Standard for the Rough Collie dates back to the 1800s. At that time, dogs were judged on a point system – so many points for each part of the dog, with the most points going to the expression and head quality. Later, this system was changed, and the Rough Collie was judged for overall balance and construction, although great importance was put upon the quality of the head and expression and, today, this is still a very important aspect of the breed.

All pedigree dogs must be registered with their national Kennel Club and every breeder of pedigree dogs must abide by the

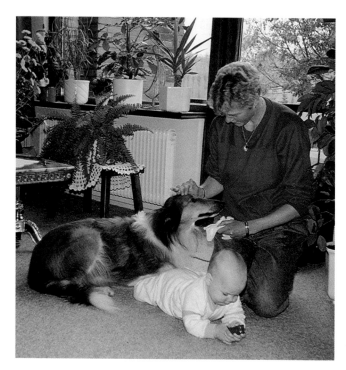

A sweet temperament and glamorous good looks makes the Rough Collie an ideal companion.

rules and regulations concerning all aspects of show dogs and dog shows. There is a Breed Standard for every breed which is a blueprint for the breed in question and a good guideline, not only for breeders and judges, but also to help the novice in choosing a puppy of their choice.

With the Standard in mind, you can get an overall picture before you set off to choose your Rough Collie, if you are a first-time buyer. First and foremost is temperament. The Rough Collie is known to be totally reliable and trustworthy with children but, having said that, no babies should ever be left alone with a dog of any breed.

SEARCH AND RESCUE

Rough Collies make excellent search and rescue dogs. They are also trained to be tracking dogs. In some countries they have to pass a temperament test before they are taken into training to assess their suitability. The Collies must be fearless and brave, showing no aggression when hearing gunfire and loud noises.

The test quite often takes place in dense forest areas and the Collie is subjected to shouting and loud gunfire. All this happens as the owner and the Collie walk along a forest path. The Collie will be allowed to bark, but he must not make any attempt to run away or show too much aggression.

The object of the test is to prove whether or not the Collie is suitable for acceptance for training as an Army, a Police or a search dog. This work is most rewarding for both the breeders and the handlers of these Collies.

THE COMMUNITY COLLIE

Your Collie can also play a very important part in the community by becoming a therapy dog. This is where Collie and owner visit residential homes and hospices, bringing comfort to the elderly who have had to part with their own beloved dogs. To be able to stroke a dog brings so much comfort to people who are ill – stroking an animal relieves stress and brings about a sense of calm. To be a therapy dog your Collie must first learn basic obedience and be able to walk calmly on the lead. He must enjoy being handled by many people.

The Rough Collie is highly-prized as a therapy dog. This is Bella, who visits nursing homes with her owner, Anne Hope.

2 Choosing Your Rough Collie

Before you take steps towards purchasing your Collie, you must consider whether it is the right dog for your way of life. Remember, a male Rough Collie will stand at least 24 inches at the shoulder, and will have an abundance of coat, with long feathering on the front legs and thick fur between the pads of the feet. All being well, and provided your Collie is healthy with no problems, he will be dependent on you for at least ten to twelve years. Most live longer than that – one of mine lived to be over 16 years old.

THE RIGHT ENVIRONMENT
Is your house big enough to keep a Rough Collie? Do you have a garden, and if you work, as most people do these days, will you have time to exercise your Collie before you leave home in the morning? Do you have a draught-free place in which to leave your Collie while you are gone? All these things must be taken into consideration before you even attempt to find your dream dog.

FINDING YOUR DREAM DOG
If you have the right environment for a Rough Collie, the next step is how to find what you are looking for in the breed. The most practical way of finding your Collie is to attend as many dog shows as you can and seek out the breeders of the type you prefer.

Rough Collies may be purchased through your local papers, but this can sometimes be a hit-and-miss affair. You can contact your national Kennel Club who will send you a list of registered breeders in your region or, with modern technology, you can surf the internet and log on to the dog section where you will find many top breeders who may have puppies for sale. Be prepared to be vetted by the breeder, as

Finding the ideal pup involves considerable research.

most will ask questions about how the puppy they have lovingly reared will be cared for.

Most breeders should also be willing to give after-care advice and to help with any problems you may encounter in the first few weeks.

Never buy the first puppy you see, unless you are absolutely sure that it is right for you. Look around and check before you buy. Always insist on seeing the mother of the pups and at least a photograph of the sire of the puppies. Ask the breeder questions about a diet chart, because one really should be provided. Find out whether the puppies have been wormed and when. It is also a good idea to ask if the stock has

been eye-tested, as eye problems can sometimes crop up in Collie breeds. Reputable breeders are proud of their stock and will be only too pleased to answer your questions.

When you have found the kennel from which you wish to purchase your Rough Collie, try not to be too impatient. Good puppies do not grow on trees. Litters are planned well in advance and the bitch in question may not come into season on time, and so the mating has to be delayed. Use this time of waiting to visit shows or agility clubs to get the feel of what it will be like when you get your own Rough Collie. Make friends with other owners, who will be just as excited as you when you show off your Rough Collie for the first time.

THE POTENTIAL SHOW PUP

Even the top breeders can sometimes get it wrong, and what was sold as a show puppy sometimes does not make the grade. All reputable kennels will be only too happy to advise you on a particular puppy's suitability for the show ring. After all, they have a reputation to uphold. But they really can only assure you that, at the time of purchase, the puppy showed promise.

DOG OR BITCH?

Before you order your Rough Collie, make sure which sex you prefer, and remember that the male Collie is two inches bigger than the female. He will also have more coat and will have more of a mane in the front than the female. If you do not want the problems of seasons that come with owning a female, then you would do well to choose a male. It is an old wives' tale that females are more loving than the male. I have always found the males to be most affectionate and very loyal.

An experienced breeder will help you to spot a pup with show potential.

When you choose your Rough Collie, you will need to decide what sex and colour you want. Left: a sable female; right: a tri-colour male.

If you want to show, I always think a male Rough Collie looks so resplendent standing with full coat in all his glory. Also, the male does not shed his fur as often as the female, who sheds after every season whether she has been mated or not. A male will also soon come back into coat after shedding it. When a female has had a litter, she is out of the show ring for at least five months. With a female you have seasons to contend with every six months, as with all females of any breed. Do you have a safe area in which to keep the bitch while she is in season, and fences to keep away stray males that can smell a bitch on heat from a great distance?

Rough Collies are not fighters and most mix very well with all breeds of dogs, and more than one male can be kept together without any trouble arising. All these things need to be talked over with the family before you embark on your venture.

WHAT COLOUR?

Rough Collies come in three beautiful colours. Sable and white means any colour sable, from bright golden to rich mahogany. A light straw colour is not desirable. A tri-colour is black, with tan on the face and legs, a white collar and, quite often, white front legs.

Blue merle is a truly magnificent colour – a marbled, almost dove-blue, with tan markings on the face and legs, a white collar and legs. This colour is one of the most difficult to produce and may cost slightly more than the other colours.

All three colours are superb and it is only a matter of individual choice. One thing I would like to mention is that, if the puppy you are about to purchase is for the show ring, then the choice of colour is not so important as the overall standard of the puppy.

ASSESSING THE LITTER

It is most important that you see the mother with her puppies. This way you will be able to ascertain the temperament of the bitch and the other puppies. If they show any problems or nervousness then, please, do beware before you buy. It is most rare that you will come across a bad-tempered Rough Collie, but it is always advisable to watch how the mother reacts, as this sometimes rubs off onto the offspring. Spend some time watching the litter at play. See if they come to you. Never take the puppy that runs away and hides, never choose a snappy puppy.

Make sure the litter looks healthy and that the puppies' coats are shiny and clean. Make sure the ears are clean, and most important, feel that the body is

The breeder will show you the mother with her puppies.

19

Watch the puppies to get an idea of their different personalities.

supple around the tummy area. If the stomach is distended and tight and the coat is harsh and staring, then, in all probability, the puppy needs worming.

COLLECTING YOUR PUPPY
The big day is here. When collecting your puppy always wear something sensible as you will need to get down to the pup's level and they will grab your trousers or tights in play.

If you are buying your puppy from a reputable breeder, he or she will have made sure that your puppy has been accustomed to household noises, such as television or radio and the noise of washing machines.

If the puppies have been born in kennels, this should not be a disadvantage to them, providing the breeders have made close and constant contact with them,

handling them often and playing with them several times a day.

Always check that the environment you collect your puppy from is scrupulously clean and do insist that you see where the pups have been kept. No caring breeder will mind, as they will have nothing to hide.

Most Rough Collie breeders are very proud of the achievements of their dogs and will only be too happy to tell you of the wins of the parents and show photographs of past generations of your puppy.

GETTING THE PAPERWORK RIGHT
Insist that you are given the puppy's Kennel Club pedigree and registration documents before you leave. Most breeders will have taken out insurance for the first six weeks of the puppy leaving their premises and this they will pass

on to you. You may then decide whether you wish to continue with the insurance company. A form will probably be sent to you before the six weeks is up, asking if you wish to continue the policy. It is advisable to take up the insurance offer as veterinary fees are quite costly should any mishap take place.

The person you buy the puppy from should be the breeder, as the breeder will be the only person entitled to register the puppies. If the puppy has had any vaccinations, you will be given a certificate along with a feeding guide and diet sheet for the puppy's first six months. Some breeders will send you off with a sample of the food your puppy has been eating. Should you wish to change the diet, please do so very carefully, following the directions given with the food, otherwise your puppy will suffer from an upset stomach.

RESCUE COLLIES

Quite often, families that lead busy lives do not have the time to train a young puppy and this is where the rescue Collie can be the answer.

It is not often that an adult Rough Collie needs rescuing but, sometimes, needs arise, and Collie Rescue associations will be most happy to help you find an adult companion that has fallen upon hard times through no fault of his own.

This is most rewarding as, quite often, a Rough Collie who has lost his owner can bring much enjoyment to a new family, thus giving not only pleasure to his new owner but giving the Collie back his lost dignity and zest for life.

It is important to see where the pups have been kept, and check the conditions are clean.

3 Care Of The New Puppy

You will already have made preparations well in advance for your new member of the family. Make sure there are no holes in the fence and that the gate has a safe lock on it, and do put a notice on your gate stating that it must always be closed.

SLEEPING ARRANGEMENTS

The next major discussion will be where will the puppy sleep. You must start as you mean to go on. If you, at first, let the puppy sleep in your room, you will have a job changing him to a kennel or a run later on. So, make some house rules – and stick to them.

Do not be tempted to let the puppy lie on your best sofa or armchairs. This is fine while the puppy is young, but think of the hair when he is a full-grown, fully-coated adult. Your furniture will be smothered, and you will certainly never be able to wear black or navy blue again!

COPING WITH INSECURITY

Once you have your puppy home, you must remember that he or she will be very insecure in the new surroundings, and may well be unsure of what is expected of him. Everything he is used to will have been taken away from him – his littermates, his mother, all the smells he is used to will all be gone.

This is one of the reasons why you must *never* buy a puppy as a Christmas present. It is so unfair, as the puppy will be pushed from place to place as the holiday season gets into full swing.

Also, the puppy's routine, such as his toilet training and regular meal times, cannot be adhered to. If your puppy is ready at Christmastime, a reputable breeder will keep the puppy for you until after the busy time is over.

If you have any other dogs or cats in the household, you must

Introductions to other pets should be dealt with calmly and sensitively.

introduce the new puppy with great care. Do not leave your puppy with other animals unless someone is at hand to intervene should any problems occur.

CREATING A PUPPY PLACE

If your Rough Collie puppy is going to live in the house, a nice draught-free area should be set aside. This can contain a good-sized plastic bed or even a large, wire cage. I find these cages most useful. Furnished with a warm vetbed or cosy blanket, the pup can curl up to sleep in it without being disturbed by anyone. It is a good idea to close the cage every so often. This way the puppy gets used to being left alone, which is very useful for when you have to go out, for you will then know that your puppy can come to no harm either from any other house-hold pets or electric cables, etc.

Never use a wicker basket. They may look nice when they are new, but they are most difficult to keep clean and soon become very tatty around the edges at teething time. If you can afford the cost, it is quite useful to put the cage inside a puppy pen. Then, when you leave the puppy overnight, you can leave newspaper down, as the puppy will not be able to go the whole night without passing water and will use the paper.

You will find most breeders paper-train puppies this way, so your puppy will be used to this. Most Rough Collies are such clean dogs and do not like to foul the area they sleep in, so this can prevent any tummy problems from occurring.

If possible, place this pen and cage where it will not be in the way and interfere with the normal running of the household.

THE FIRST NIGHT

Most puppies, on arrival to a new home, will find this a traumatic time. You must remember that he has left his brothers and sisters, and the first night away from the only family he has known will be quite distressful and he may cry when left alone. This is where you have to make decisions and act as you mean to go on.

If you keep getting up to go to the puppy, he will expect this all the time. You must be sensible. Make sure the puppy is warm and comfortable, and has a toy to curl up with such as an old teddy bear, or any soft toy that he cannot harm himself on. Then you can rest, knowing the puppy will soon settle down to sleep once he realises no one is going to come every time he cries. It is advisable to check on the soft toy you leave with the puppy, making sure that it does not have any eyes that can be taken out and chewed. It is also sensible to remove the squeaker inside any rubber toys as these can so easily be swallowed.

A ticking clock near to his bed may help, or even a covered, stone hot water-bottle – never use a rubber one as this can so easily be chewed.

HOUSETRAINING

Puppies, like babies, go to the toilet more often than adults and it is a good idea to train your puppy as soon as possible, using words like "wee wees".

A crate provides a safe, comfortable place in which to put your puppy.

Taking your puppy out frequently will make housetraining a quick and simple procedure.

I know it sounds silly, but most dogs will perform and soon learn to go to the toilet on command. When your puppy goes on command, give him plenty of praise immediately, and in no time he will be housetrained.

Puppies will want to go to the toilet as soon as they wake up, and as soon as they have eaten. Keep to a routine as much as possible and train your puppy by tone of voice. You will be surprised how quickly a Rough Collie learns. The sooner you start, the better – and you will end up with a well-behaved adult dog as a result.

THE PUPPY'S DAY AND DIET

A simple routine is easy to keep to and I suggest the following for your new puppy.

When you get up, take your puppy outside, even if he has already relieved himself on the paper.

The following diet is for puppies of 8 to 12 weeks – but *do remember* to follow the diet sheet that you have been given by the breeder in the early days, and only change it with great care.

Breakfast: about a quarter of a pint of milk mixed with any type of easily digestible cereal or porridge. Then take the puppy outside and stay with him until he has performed his toilet. This is a good idea as you can check the puppy's stools to see if he is loose (the correct stool should be firm but moist and easy to pick up).

CARE OF THE NEW PUPPY

The puppy can then have about 15 minutes' play time and then be taken to his bed for a rest period. Young puppies sleep for quite long periods and it is important to let the puppy sleep if he is to grow properly.

Lunch: 4 to 5 oz of minced, raw meat mixed with the same amount of well-soaked puppy biscuit, or you can use a good-quality mixer adapted for puppies. You may, of course, wish to use one of the many dry foods available for puppies. In this case, always read the label and use according to instructions for the breed and age of puppy.

Again, take the puppy outside to relieve himself, followed by play time. Then back to his bed again.

While you are playing with your puppy, now is the time to start gentle training, beginning with calling his name. If he comes, give him a little treat and tell him what a good boy he is.

Tea time: you may wish to feed the same as lunch, but by way of a change, you can introduce other foods such as scrambled eggs or cooked fish and rice, or even cooked chicken but, please, do take care that these foods contain no bones.

Take the puppy outside again,

Routine is very important for a young puppy.

Your pup should be fed the diet recommended by the breeder.

using the same procedure. **Supper:** any milky cereal or porridge, outside again, and so to bed.

Just before you go to bed take your puppy out one last time, put paper down overnight and this way your puppy will soon be housetrained.

You will need to increase the diet as the puppy grows, and if you are feeding a diet that is homemade, you will need to incorporate some form of vitamin supplement daily. Popular is calcium with vitamin D but if you feed an all-in-one diet you will not need to use any supplements at all.

Do check daily that your puppy is clean, his fur soft and shiny, and his body soft and fleshy. If the coat is hard and staring and has no shine, it is a sure sign that the puppy needs worming. If you are unsure how to worm your puppy, your vet will do it for you at a very small cost.

As your puppy grows he will not need milk so much, and if you are feeding an all-in-one diet, he should not need any at all.

If, after feeding, your puppy has loose bowel motions, then it is one of three things – the food does not agree with him, or he has eaten too much, or he is not well. To eliminate the first two, starve the puppy for one day and then feed him a very light diet such as chicken and rice for a few days, and if all is well then, in all probability, whatever you fed him previously did not agree with him. However, if the puppy is still loose, then you must consult your vet.

VACCINATIONS AND WORMING

It is advisable to take your puppy along to your local surgery as soon as possible and register him. Your vet will tell you when he can be vaccinated and will inform you of a worming programme. When going to the vet's surgery for the first time, *please do not* put your puppy on the floor where other dogs have walked; remember, he has had no vaccinations and will be at risk from infection.

Until your puppy has been vaccinated you must not take him to the park or walk him through the streets, but there is no reason why you should not indulge in a short car ride for a change of scenery. This will get your puppy used to journeys and there is nothing a Collie loves better than jumping into the car for a ride to the park. All Rough Collies love to travel.

Your vaccinations will consist of Canine Distemper, Hepatitis, Parvovirus, Kennel Cough and Leptospirosis. If you wish to put your dog into boarding kennels, or take him to ringcraft or agility classes, unless your dog has been vaccinated against these diseases, they will not take him.

EARLY TRAINING

During the time leading up to the day your puppy can face the outside world, it is a good idea to do a little training of your own.

LEAD-TRAINING

Firstly, put a collar on for short

Lead-training sessions should be kept short.

periods. Next, attach a lead to it and try a little walk around the garden. Some puppies take to this with no problems, but others have been known to dig their heels in and refuse to move. Some act as though they are being murdered so, at this stage, you need to have patience. Have a bag or a pocket with treats in, and use some gentle coaxing, and in no time at all everything soon comes together. If the puppy thinks it is a game, he will soon learn.

Restrict your puppy's exercise to the garden until he has had his vaccinations.

Never drag your puppy or use harsh words; this is not the right way to train your puppy. Be gentle, using words of praise and calling your Collie by name, and after a few days your puppy will respond and begin to enjoy the walks in the garden. Then, when the vaccinations are completed, you can venture out for short walks.

Never over-exercise your puppy. Up until he is six months old just keep to short, gentle walks near to home. This way your puppy will feel secure in the knowledge that each time he goes out, he will return to his familiar surroundings. This builds up confidence for both you and your puppy, helping to build a good relationship. A Collie that walks calmly by your side is a pleasure and it is nice when people compliment you on your puppy's good behaviour, giving you a sense of pride in a job well done.

SIT

Show your pup a treat in one hand, and hold it just above his nose so he has to sit in order to reach the treat. With your other hand, gently push his hindquarters down. When he sits, give him the treat, say Sit and give your Collie pup lots of praise. Keep practising until your clever pup will Sit immediately, as soon as you ask him to.

DOWN

The same principle is used for Down. Firstly, tell your pup to Sit, then show him a treat, and hold it on the floor in front of the pup so he must lay down to reach it. If he doesn't understand what is required, you can gently slide his paws forward so his Sit becomes a Down. You should only do this a couple of times, as your pup will soon understand what he needs to do. As before, as soon as he goes Down, say "Down", give him a treat, and lots of praise and petting.

Lure your pup into the Sit position with a tasty treat.

COME

As stated earlier, you should already have taught your puppy his name, and to have introduced basic recall – where the pup is given a treat whenever he comes to you. Keep practising this exercise, increasing the level of difficulty gradually. For example, slowly extend the distance from which you call your pup; ask him to come to you from one room to another, etc. Always praise him, and show him you are very pleased to see him when he comes to you.

STAY

Put your pup in a Sit position, say "Stay" firmly, take one step back, wait a second, then return to your pup. Praise him and give him a reward for waiting – even if it was only for a second! Next time, take two steps back, and make him wait two seconds. Gradually increase the distance and time, but do not do too much too soon – the Stay exercise should be done slowly but thoroughly.

HOME ALONE

In today's world, most people work and, although it is unfair to leave a puppy for any length of time, possibly arrangements can be made with a neighbour to look

Although the challenges of puppyhood will be over, the junior Collie still has specific needs which must be attended to.

after your puppy while it is young. Alternatively, you can make an outside run and kennel for your puppy. This must be warm and draught-free and your puppy must be left with plenty of drinking water and something to occupy his mind.

I would never sell a puppy to anyone who worked full-time but, for someone who is only away for a few hours, this should not be a problem. If you have trained your puppy to be left on his own for a few hours at a time, all should be well.

Most Rough Collies are not destructive. If you do not have a kennel and run, as long as you have a place in your home where you can leave him safely, away from any loose electric wires or ends of carpet that stick out, all should be well.

THE JUNIOR COLLIE
You have got through the first six months and are now sighing with relief that all has gone according to plan. By now, you should have a well-adjusted young dog.

The youngster will now be on two main meals and a light supper. If your Collie is too thin, increase his main meal; if too fat, reduce accordingly. I like to feed a small breakfast with the main meal in the early evening but, however you feed, always make sure that you stick to your routine times, this way you can avoid upset stomachs and not upset the Collie's digestive system.

At around four to five months your Collie will be teething and sometimes this can be quite painful, so babies' teething jelly can be very useful. The Collie's mouth will be quite sore and some good, hard, rawhide chews, or a raw marrowbone, will help, as the Collie will want to chew on something and a bone will be far better than your best shoes.

While your puppy is teething, keep checking to see how the teeth are coming through. Most Collies do not have any problems with double teeth, but there could always be a first time. If you have purchased your Rough Collie as a show dog, the time of teething could be a very tricky time. The pain of the teeth pushing through the gums quite often causes the dog's ears to prick up and this should be watched with great care. If your Collie has pricked ears for more than one day you must massage the ear tips with some cream to keep them soft and supple. This is a trying time, as you will not be able to show a Rough Collie with ears that stand up, so do watch this stage of development with care.

Pups and young dogs need plenty of safe toys to chew.

33

4 General Care And Training

Rough Collies are a very healthy breed and can live to be quite old – as I have said I had one who lived to be almost 17 years old. Most Collies are about 12 or 13 years old before they begin to slow down, so remember this when you set out to buy your Collie.

DIET

Rough Collies reach maturity at about one year and at this stage they require only one meal a day. However, all the Rough Collies I know like a small breakfast and look forward to this meal every day. There are two schools of thought on feeding and no two dogs are ever the same. So, the choice of diet is in your hands and you must use what you feel is best, not only for your Collie but also for your budget.

The diet that takes more time is the meat/tripe and biscuit regime. I have never known any Collie to turn their nose up at tripe. The smell is not pleasant, but most long-standing breeders use it as a main meal. It is quite readily available in good pet shops and can be bought in one-pound packets for easy thawing. An adult dog that has come to full development can live quite happily on an equal ratio of tripe and biscuit, or tripe and mixer, whichever you prefer.

Many busy owners tend to feed an all-in-one diet, or tinned food. There are so many to choose from that you can be spoilt for choice. If you are going to use tinned food do make sure that you mix it with the correct amount of mixer or biscuit, otherwise it can affect your Collie's digestive system. Some expensive foods may be too rich and have too much protein for an adult dog, so do read the labels. You only have to look at your dog to see if you are getting it right because it will show, not only in the condition of coat, and the bright eyes, but also in the dog's temperament.

It is vital that fresh water should be available at all times and that the drinking bowl is cleaned every day.

If he is under the weather at any time, or if he has grown old, a light diet will be more beneficial, such as chicken and rice or scrambled eggs. Cooked fish is also very nourishing but do make sure no bones are present in the fish or chicken. If your dog goes off his food for more than two days, a trip to the vet would be in order, as Collies are quite good feeders and will sometimes eat even if they are not well.

Your Collie pup must get used to being groomed from a young age.

GROOMING

You must make your Collie stand to be groomed at least once a week. This is a vital part of his training which starts as early as when he is in the nest with his brothers and sisters. Hopefully, your Collie should be used to this by the time you purchase him.

You will need the following tools:

- A very good-quality brush. It is well worth investing in a pure bristle brush. They may be expensive but a good brushing will stimulate a dog's skin and get rid of any dead hair. A wire brush, or a cheaper nylon version, may tear the coat and leave dead, brittle ends.
- A fine tooth comb, with teeth of about $\frac{1}{16}$th of an inch.
- A wide tooth comb with teeth of about $\frac{1}{8}$th of an inch.
- Scissors, about 6 inches and tapered.
- Scissors with blunt or rounded ends, for trimming between the feet.
- Nail cutters.

Through regular brushing, the coat will not become matted or

GROOMING
Pauline Skyrme with Emryks Heavenly Bliss

Ready for grooming.

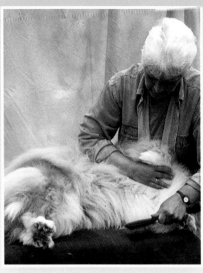

Lie the dog on his side to groom his undercarriage.

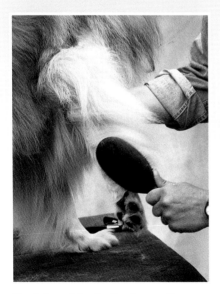

Don't forget the feathering on the forelegs.

The hindquarters should be brushed thoroughly.

The chest hair is profuse and will need considerable attention.

Comb around the ears.

Trim the hair from the pads.

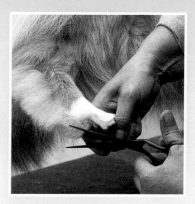

The feathering will need tidying up.

The finished product.

tangled. There is nothing sadder than an unkempt Collie, whether it is a show dog or just a family companion. Regular brushing at least twice a week is most important.

Start from the back and work your way slowly to the front, leaving the large mane and collar to the last. Brush upwards towards the tail, making sure that the underside of the tail is given a good brush or comb through. Then brush over the loin and back, never forgetting the elbows and under the belly, and the feathering on the front legs. Brush the mane upwards at first and then smooth it downwards, which gives a beautiful, groomed outline. Then do the huge collar. Lastly, comb around the base of the ears and remove any dead hair that spoils the ear outline. You can do this with finger and thumb or with thinning scissors.

If the hair on the back hock is very thick and unsightly, take the tapered scissors and very carefully trim off the unwanted hair. Before you attempt to do this, first use your comb to separate the fur. Comb upwards away from the foot, trim lightly, making sure to leave at least a quarter of an inch of hair on the hock. If you cut this too short, it will give the appearance of skinny back legs.

Do trim a little at a time until you are satisfied that both back legs have equal amounts of fur. If the hair is very thick on the hock, you may thin some of this out with the thinning scissors prior to actually cutting.

A few years ago, exhibitors were allowed to use whitener or chalk to enhance the white parts of the Collie, but this is no longer allowed and anyone taking a Collie in the ring with any enhancer on the coat could end up being banned from exhibiting.

In the USA many breeders trim the ears and also cut away the whiskers from the muzzle. I, personally, find it hardens the expression if too much hair is trimmed from the ears. Some Collies may have excessive hair around the base of the ear and this may be carefully stripped out with finger and thumb. Arrange the ear as it would look when the Collie is alert, then comb the hair on the back of the ears towards the outside edge and either pluck with finger and thumb, or use thinning scissors to take off any hair that spoils the ear shape. If you are not sure how to do this, ask a Collie person to advise you. Never take any hair off the tip of the ear that folds over, and remember, over-stripping can cause a perfect ear carriage to go pricked.

A well-groomed Collie is a wonderful sight and it is so easy to keep a Collie in good order. One of the most rewarding pleasures of owning a Rough Collie is the grooming sessions. I find it so relaxing to sit on the floor, brushing my Collies. Any stress you had before starting will soon have gone by the time you have finished. The Collies love it too.

CHECKING THE COAT

This grooming session is also a good time to look deep into the undercoat to detect any unwanted visitors, or skin disease that can be swiftly nipped in the bud. Collies have a double coat. The undercoat is soft and thick and very woolly. This gives good insulation against all weathers, be it hot or cold. The top coat is long, hiding the undercoat completely. To tell if your Collie has a good, weatherproof coat, go out in the rain. A good, harsh, well-fitting jacket that is correct for the Collie will be wet on the top but bone-dry underneath. A poor coat will be soaked right down to the skin.

TEETH

From an early age it is advisable to check and clean the dog's teeth. This is a simple task and, if you start early enough, your Collie will soon get used to having it done. There is nothing worse than judging a Collie that you have admired standing and moving, to find that the teeth are dirty and foul smelling. Once or twice a week, brush your Collie's teeth with a good-quality brush, or use one of the very useful finger brushes and obtain toothpaste from your vet.

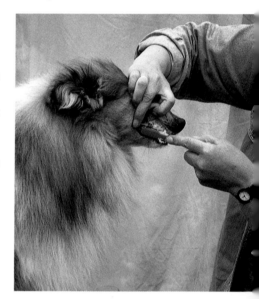

A weekly brush will keep your Collie's teeth clean, and his breath fresh.

EARS

Due to the semi-erect shape of the Rough Collie's ears, there should be no health problems there. The shape of the ear allows air to penetrate but, sometimes, mites get into the ears, especially if you keep cats, so it is a good idea to check ears once a week. Never poke anything down the ears. Use a good cleaner, which you can obtain from your vet, that will bring all the debris to the surface, making it easy to wipe away.

NAILS

Most Rough Collies will wear down their nails naturally, especially if they are kept on hard ground or road-walked. Most dogs hate having their nails clipped, so it is a good idea to start young. Do handle the feet often. Most puppies, until they are older and can get out on to a hard surface, will need to have the nails cut every two or three weeks. They soon become used to having the nails cut but, even then, some will find it traumatic, so this is where you exercise your control. However, if all else fails and you cannot cut the dog's nails, then a visit to the vet's once a month will have to do. It is very rare that a Rough Collie would ever bite but,

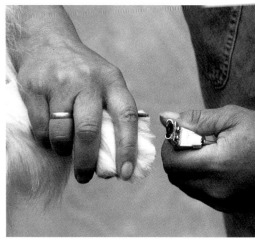

Nails should be checked regularly, and trimmed if necessary.

in a situation where the Collie refuses to have his nails cut and gives off the odd growl, it is advisable to use a muzzle or, if one is not available, tie a stocking around his nose. This safeguards dog and handler.

If you need to trim the excess fur between the pads of the feet, do take great care and make sure someone is on hand to help if needed. The hair can sometimes become thick and lumpy, which makes the toes spread. This can be most uncomfortable for the dog. Take the foot in your hand and then, using a pair of blunt-ended scissors, trim the hair between the pads of the feet, taking great care not to go too close to the skin.

Only take off the untidy hair around the edge of the feet, as this will give a nice rounded appearance.

BATHING

A Rough Collie is normally a very clean dog and does not need bathing too often. Twice a year will be sufficient unless, of course, he has been out in the mud. Then all that is needed is to wash the underbelly, legs and feet.

If you have to bath your Rough Collie, do make sure that you have a rubber mat in the bottom of the bath. This will prevent the dog from slipping and also stop the bath from being scratched.

Make sure you have everything to hand before you start. Never leave a Collie in a bath unattended. Check that you have a good dog shampoo (never use human shampoo on a dog) and plenty of towels. Some human help would also not be a bad idea as a Rough Collie can be heavy when wet.

Put a little water in the bottom of the bath, with the plug in, so the dog's feet are just immersed in the water. Pour over water from a jug or shower head and slowly massage in the shampoo, making sure you get right down to the skin. If your Rough Collie has the correct harsh coat, this could take a little while to lather up. When well-soaked and soapy, massage the coat well, taking great care not to get the shampoo in the dog's eyes. Five minutes of lathering should be ample time. Then start rinsing and make sure you get every last drop of shampoo off of the coat. Keep rinsing until the water is clear. Remove the bath plug before you start rinsing to make sure the feet and legs are not left soapy.

Remove surplus water with your hands and, before your Collie can give a big shake, cover him with towels and gently rub him as dry as you can before removing him from the bath. Then take him outside where, I can assure you, he will shake the rest of the water out. All that is left to do is to blow-dry him with a dryer, grooming out at the same time, or grooming him after he has dried naturally. Pay special attention to the hair behind the ears as this can quite often knot up and, if not checked, end up matted.

The best time to bath your Collie is when he is moulting; it gets rid of all the dead hairs and he will come back into coat much more quickly.

Rough Collies are generally healthy and long-lived. This 8-month-old (left) and 11½-year-old (right) enjoy many of the same activities.

THE OLDER COLLIE

Like all of us, as your Collie gets older, he will probably become arthritic and it is important that he has a soft, warm, fleecy bed to lie on at night. Make sure that he sleeps in a draught-free area and that his coat is dry before he settles down for the night. In fact you should never let your Rough Collie, whatever his age, go to bed with a wet coat.

Gentle exercise and good food, maybe giving three small meals instead of one big meal, are essential. Remember that the diet he had when young is now no longer suitable, and he will need smaller meals of a more nourishing nature. Never give food straight from the fridge,

slightly warm it to make it more palatable. Scrambled eggs, chicken or fish with rice, or boiled lamb and rice, make a tasty meal for an older dog that sometimes may not have a good appetite. If you like to feed tinned food, there are many low-protein diets available that will be suitable for the older dog.

An old dog cannot tolerate extremes of temperature so never leave your old Collie out on a wet and windy day, or a very hot day, unless there is some shelter.

Your Collie's mouth may smell, so it is a good idea to check that the teeth are still intact and there is no evidence of mouth tumours.

Why not raise the dog's water bowl from the ground to make life a little easier. It may hurt his neck and back, if he is arthritic, if he has to stoop low for a drink. If your Collie's joints become painful, have a chat with your vet, who will give some pills to ease the pain of arthritic joints.

If your old Collie should lose his eyesight do not worry too much, as he will be able to cope well, providing you do not change the layout of the home he knows so well.

The Rough Collie is a very proud dog and you must respect the fact that he would not like to lose his dignity. Therefore, when the time comes when you have to make a decision, please do so before he loses all his faculties and remember that this decision is the best and final act of love you can give your Collie. Remember the good times. The lovely walks, the nights sitting round the fire vying for the best spot, and give thanks for all the pleasure this wonderful breed of dog has given you.

ESSENTIAL TRAINING

Most Rough Collies are so eager to please that they learn very quickly. It is essential that you take basic training classes in order to teach your dog to "Sit", to "Stay" and to "Come" (see Chapter Three). In an emergency, when you shout "Sit" your Collie should do so at once. Many an accident has been averted through simple

Continue your pup's training into his adulthood.

basic training. There is also nothing better than a well-behaved dog.

There are plenty of activities your Rough Collie can take part in – Tracking/Working Trials, Agility, Obedience, etc. But, before going on to these bigger things, you must first join a club that can offer you and your Collie the type of training you have chosen.

To find a club that specialises in the type of training you want, simply obtain this information from your national Kennel Club, or from any other dog owner you may meet. Your vet's surgery will also know where the local clubs are and at what time and on what day they meet.

Obedience (below) and tracking (above) are just some of the sports you can get involved in.

Leaping the tyre.

AGILITY

Agility is a fun obstacle course which must be completed quickly and accurately. Dogs love it – especially the lively and intelligent Rough Collie.

The following training tips (courtesy of Enid Binns from The Rough and Smooth Collie Training Association) will help you – and your Collie – enjoy Agility to the full.

- Give your Collie lots of play from an early age. Run around with your dog on your left and your right (but not as close as you would for Obedience).

- Use toys and/or treats, together with your voice, to get your Collie interested and keen.
- Don't bore your Collie with too much repetition – end training sessions while you are both still enjoying yourselves.
- Give lots of praise.
- Reward your Collie for correct actions and ignore incorrect ones.
- Find a training club where training methods for different breeds are practised – not where all dogs are treated as if they are Border Collies.
- Above all, keep training fun!

Through the rigid tunnel.

Over the hurdles.

5 *Showing Your Rough Collie*

Going to a dog show is great fun and is a hobby for thousands of dog lovers. If you intend to show your Rough Collie, it is a good idea to attend ringcraft classes which will help both of you to learn the basic art of dog showing. It is also a good plan to go to dog shows to see how dogs are shown in the ring and to join one of the many Rough Collie breed clubs which exist throughout the world.

Before you can exhibit your Collie, you must make sure that he is obedient and can walk in a calm way on the lead. He must also be able to stand quietly. Ringcraft classes get your Collie used to being handled and having his mouth and teeth examined in the same way as if he were at a show. You can make your Collie look more alert, and bring the ears to attention, by offering a treat or rustling a bag. Always keep a few tasty bits of liver or cheese in your pocket while training; these are great rewards if given along with much praise.

Frequent practice will make the show stance second nature to your Collie.

Your Collie will be examined closely by the judge.

A successful show dog should be focused and attentive in the ring.

Teach your Collie how to move on a loose lead. If he pulls forward, or breaks stride, gently jerk back on the lead and then give praise when the dog is in the correct position. Keep the lessons short but go through the routine every day. As you progress you will find you and your Collie forming a bond that will always be there.

As you become more confident, go through the actions of being at a show and move your Collie in a triangle, then straight up and down, bringing the dog back to the starting point. Finish up with the dog standing four-square and at this point touch your pocket – your Collie knows this is where

you keep the treats and will respond by bringing up his ears in an alert manner, thus giving an overall picture of an alert and attentive Collie.

If you enjoy this and think your Collie has the makings of a show dog, now is the time to look around for some small shows to go to. This could be the start of a very rewarding hobby. However, showing can be expensive, and it is essential that you are honest about your dog. If you are going to show your Rough Collie you will need to be conversant with the Breed Standard, the blueprint for the breed, as set out by your national Kennel Club. Do you know the Breed Standard requirements and does your dog fit them?

A GUIDE TO THE BREED STANDARDS

As with any breed, one of the most important factors is temperament, and the Rough Collie should at all times show a friendly disposition with no trace of aggressiveness or nervousness. The head and skull of the Rough Collie is of great importance but the overall construction of the dog should not be sacrificed for the sake of a beautiful head.

THE HEAD The Rough Collie should have a long and lean head, with a flat skull and, when viewed from the front or in profile, should resemble a clean wedge with a slight but perceptible stop midway between the top of the skull and the end of the nose. There should be a well-rounded muzzle and a good under-jaw.

EYES The eye placement of the Collie determines the expression, and this is most important on the Rough Collie. A very small eye gives the appearance of a mean and shifty look. An eye that is too large gives a dull and stupid expression. The shape should be an open almond and set obliquely, this is to enable the Collie to have full vision. The eye colour should

The muzzle should be well rounded, with a good under-jaw.

always be dark brown, except in the blue merle Collie, and then it may be blue, or one blue one brown, but never wall-eyed, as sometimes seen in the Old English Sheepdog. The eyes of the Rough Collie must be sweet and dreamy, yet full of intelligence with a quick alertness when listening.

EARS In order to achieve the correct expression, the placement and size of the Rough Collie's ears is of great importance. The ears should be small, not too close together, and yet not too far apart, and set on top of the skull. When the Collie is resting, they are carried thrown back, but when he is alert they are carried forward and semi-erect. This means that approximately two thirds of the ear is standing erect, with the top third tipping forward in a natural bend. This, together with the soft intelligent eye placement, gives the desired expression that is so important in this breed.

MOUTH The teeth should be of good size, and have a complete scissor bite. That means the upper teeth closely overlap the lower teeth and are set square in a strong jaw.

The neck should have a profuse mane which frames the head.

NECK The neck of the Rough Collie should be well-arched, muscular and of a fair length. The neck should have profuse fur and a mane that frames the face.

FOREQUARTERS The front of the Rough Collie should have sloping, well-angulated shoulders and the front legs should be straight and muscular, not in or out at the elbows. Moderate bone structure should be in keeping with the overall construction of the dog.

BODY The body should be slightly long, compared with the dog's height. The chest should be deep and the ribs well-sprung, giving plenty of heart room. The back should be firm with a slight rise over the loins.

HINDQUARTERS The hindlegs should be muscular at the thighs, clean and smooth below, with well-bent stifle and strong, well let-down hocks. This is to enable the Collie to move with purpose and drive.

FEET The feet should be oval with the soles well-padded, the toes arched and close together. Hindfeet are slightly less arched but never flat and splayed.

TAIL This should be long and reach at least to the hock joint. It is carried low when the dog is quiet and may have a slight upward swirl at the tip.

It may be carried gaily when the dog is excited but must never be carried over the back (Spitz-like).

COAT The coat should fit the outline of the body and be dense. The outer coat is straight and harsh and the undercoat is soft and very close, almost hiding the skin. The mane and front frill should be very abundant, but the mask and face must be smooth.

The dense coat should fit the outline of the body.

The three Rough Collie colours: blue merle (left), sable and white (below, left) and tri-colour (below, right).

The ears should be smooth at the tips and carry more hair at the base. The back of the front legs should be well-feathered, the hind legs smooth below the hock, and the hair on the tail should be very profuse.

MOVEMENT This is a distinct characteristic of the breed and a dog that is of sound construction should never be out at the elbow, yet should move with front feet comparatively close together. Plaiting, or a rolling movement, is highly undesirable. The hind legs from hock joint to ground, when viewed from the rear, should be parallel but not too close; when viewed from the side, the action should be smooth with a reasonably long stride and should appear light and effortless. The hind legs should be powerful, giving good driving action.

COLOUR As stated earlier, the Rough Collie comes in three colours, the most popular being the sable and white. This ranges from a bright golden red to a deep mahogany, and in some cases a dark-shaded sable (although this colour is not seen so much these days). A pale, straw-blonde colour is highly undesirable.

The movement should be light and effortless.

Tri-colour: The main coat is black with tan markings on eyebrows and cheeks, also tan markings on the legs and feet. A rusty tinge to the coat is undesirable.

Blue Merle: The main coat is of a silvery blue which is splashed and marbled with black. The blue must be clear, and the black markings should not be excessive. Rich tan markings on the face and legs are preferred but if absent should not be penalised.

55

White markings: All the above colours should carry the typical white Collie markings to a greater or lesser degree. The following markings are favourable: white collar (full or part), white front legs and feet, and a white tip to the tail. A blaze may be carried on the face. The white should not go beyond the shoulder, or above the hock, and there should be no white patches on the main part of the body – this is classed as white factoring and is highly undesirable.

SIZE Males: 56-61 cms (22-24 ins) at the shoulder. Females: 51-56 cms (20-22 ins) at the shoulder.

MAKING A CHAMPION

Dog shows differ from country to country. To become a Champion in the United States and Canada, your dog must win a total of fifteen points under a minimum of three different judges, including two major shows under different judges. Five points is the maximum that can be won at any show.

All the countries who are affiliated to the Fédération Cynologique Internationale (FCI) must adhere to the rules laid down by this governing body. The judging differs in that each dog entered must be judged on its own merits and the owner given a written critique before leaving the ring. The rules about becoming a National Champion (CAC) also differ. In the Scandinavian countries, a dog cannot be a full Champion until he has passed a

Showing is an absorbing hobby.

very stringent temperament test.

To become an International Champion, a dog must win four CACIBs (Certificate d'Aptitude Internationale Beauté) in three different countries and two of these must be won in the country where the dog resides. Also the CACIBs must be won under different judges.

To become an Australian Champion, a Collie must amass 100 points at shows, plus four Challenge Certificates (CCs) under four different judges.

In Northern Ireland the judging system is the same as in the UK. Southern Ireland is affiliated with the FCI and dogs there can now win CACIB/CAC and go across the border to win CCs.

In the UK, there are a variety of shows that differ from the rest of the world. There are Matches, which are held under Kennel Club rules. There are Exemption shows, which are exempt from Kennel Club rules but a special licence from the KC is still needed to hold the show. Sanction shows are restricted to twenty classes only,

and confined to members of a club. Limited shows are also for club members but there are usually more classes on offer, mainly variety classes.

Open shows are open to all pedigree dogs, and you do not need to be a member, but all dogs must be registered with the Kennel Club. At this type of show the more popular breeds such as the Collie would be given their own four classes.

Then there are the Championship shows, which are very competitive. It is at this type of show that Challenge Certificates are on offer and Champions are made up. At these shows you can also qualify for entry to Crufts Championship show, the UK premiere event of the year. In order to become a UK Champion, a dog must be awarded three CCs under three different judges. A dog can only gain its title when it is twelve months of age. Unlike other countries, the CC winner can come from any class of the day that has CCs on offer for their breed.

6 *Breeding From Your Collie*

If you are thinking about breeding from your Collie, do give it considerable thought before you embark on such a programme.

THE STUD DOG

You may wish, at some time, to offer your Collie at stud. Unless he is a top winner this is most inadvisable because, having once been used at stud, your Collie will always be on the lookout for a bitch on heat, and I can assure you this can be a problem.

Your Collie will not miss anything by not being used at stud and, unless you know what you are doing, harm may come to him, or to the bitch that has come to call. If you insist on letting him mate a bitch, then do get professional help from another knowledgeable Collie person. Never attempt such a mating without help.

THE BROOD BITCH

If you have a bitch, you may want

Breeding should never be attempted unless the quality of the parents is assured.

to breed from her at some stage, and although this is very rewarding, it also has its pitfalls. You must make sure you have the money to carry out the breeding programme. Stud fees are not cheap. Then you must have a secure, quiet place for her in which to have the puppies. You must have money put by in case of an emergency, such as for vet's fees. Then there are the puppies who will need special food and warmth. If you work, you will have to take time off, as the bitch will not be able to be left on her own, either prior to the birth or until after the puppies are at least six weeks old. You must also make sure you find suitable buyers for the puppies.

PREPARATIONS

If you are not put off by the above sermon then I suggest you go back to the breeder from whom you purchased your Collie and ask for advice. Make sure the bitch you intend to breed from is not overweight, that she has been wormed and that her vaccinations are up to date prior to the mating.

Have her eyes tested and her hips scored, and check that the dog you use has also had the relevant tests.

THE MATING

When your Collie is due in season, watch her every day to try to find out day one of the season. The normal time for mating is around the thirteenth and fifteenth day, but not every bitch is the same.

Your Collie will not stand for

the dog until she is ready and that can be from day seven onwards. When she is ready she will lift her tail and, sometimes, flirt with the dog. At this stage it is most important for one person to hold the bitch while another attends to the dog. The reason for this is that if the bitch suddenly objects, or tries to sit down, help is at hand. Sometimes a mating only takes a few minutes, yet also be prepared for a long tie. This is when the bitch holds the dog, using her internal muscles, and the dog cannot release himself until the bitch relaxes and then releases the dog. Some dogs like to turn back-to-back and can stand like this for quite a considerable time.

Once your bitch has been mated, she may go looking for another mate, so keep her well away from any parks or any place where she could meet another dog until her vulva has reduced and she has no discharge.

THE PREGNANT BITCH

There is no need to change her diet or routine for at least five weeks. After this time it is advisable to make sure your bitch has good, nourishing food. Years ago, it was the norm to increase calcium levels when a bitch was in whelp but, of

A whelping box is an essential piece of equipment.

late, most vets have discounted this as it has been known to bring about inertia, a condition which prevents the bitch from having normal contractions.

Before you give your bitch any additives, ask the advice of your vet.

Towards the eighth week, change from one, or two, large meals a day, to three smaller meals, as a bitch can become very uncomfortable as she becomes heavier in whelp. Do not over-exercise her, but let her have gentle walks up until it is time for her to give birth. It is important that the bitch has been shown where she is due to whelp and, during the last week, has been left in the area to become familiar with her new surroundings.

ARRANGEMENTS FOR WHELPING

You will, of course, have prepared her whelping box a few weeks prior to the date the pups are due and have introduced the bitch to her new surroundings well in advance. The items you will require for the whelping are as follows:

- Sterile scissors.
- A large bowl of warm water containing antiseptic, for cleansing your hands.
- If possible, some artery forceps, to cut through the umbilical cord if the bitch does not chew through it herself.
- Calcium with vitamin D.
- Permanganate of potash, which is available from chemists, and is to be used if the umbilical cord bleeds too much. A little, placed on the head of a cotton bud, soon stops the bleeding.
- Disposable gloves.
- Paper towels.
- Warm dry towels.
- Kitchen scales for weighing the pups.

- A cardboard box with a hot water bottle or heat pad in it. This is in case you need to transfer the pups to the vet in the event of complications.
- Plenty of newspaper.
- Some clean, fluffy veterinary bedding.
- A never-ending supply of coffee for yourself.
- And, most important, your vet's telephone number and a car that will start if needed.

If your Collie is in full coat it may be as well to cut off, or tie back, her long petticoats. Bandage up the tail, as it will become increasingly wet and a puppy may strangle in the long, wet fur.

THE BIG DAY

The normal gestation period is 63 days but it is not unusual for a maiden bitch to go into labour on the 57th day. As the day draws near, it is advisable to start taking your Collie's temperature twice daily. The average temperature of a dog is 101 degrees but, around 24 hours prior to whelping, the temperature will drop to 98 degrees F.

Make sure the thermometer is not thin or brittle. The end with the mercury in must be thick and rounded. The thermometer should be well-shaken, down to 96 degrees F or less. Then insert the mercury end, covered in a little vaseline if you wish, into the dog's rectum until at least half of the thermometer has been inserted. On no account use force. If you have a problem, alter the position. When inserted correctly, leave for one minute, making sure that you are holding the end at all times. If the temperature is over 102 degrees F, it may be advisable to call your vet.

At this stage the bitch will want to pass water frequently, and she will become quite agitated and tear up the paper in her box. She is best left alone, as she will be nesting and preparing herself for the birth.

However, do check on her, every half-hour, to see if she has gone into the second stage of labour, which is when the lips of the vulva will soften and protrude. As the time draws near, she will become increasingly restless. She will continue to scratch up her bed and to pant heavily. She may also refuse all food.

SECOND STAGE

At the next stage of labour, the bitch will tremble and look glazed about the eyes. The cervix will

Most Rough Collie bitches make wonderful mothers.

dilate, a watery discharge can be seen and, as the contractions become stronger, she will pant a great deal and become very restless.

The bitch will continue to push harder with each contraction. As whelping continues you will see a pale green, watery discharge; this is quite normal. The contractions will become stronger and more frequent. The water bag is the first thing to be seen; it appears as a skin-like bulb. At this stage do not touch the sac. The fluid inside the bag is protecting the puppy from outside pressure.

The membrane will burst, followed by the puppy. If all is well, the bitch will then tear the sac herself, releasing the puppy. If the bitch does not tear the sac to release the pup, then you must do it for her. Using finger and thumb, gently tear away the sac from the puppy, who will appear attached to the placenta and the umbilical cord.

As the puppy emerges, the bitch will want to take over and she will bite the cord. If she chews the cord too short, just dab a small amount of potash on to the stump to stop the bleeding.

If your bitch does not chew the cord, you will have to squash the artery forceps together, about two inches (5 cms) from the belly, and tear away the rest of the placenta with your finger and thumb.

Make sure there is no mucus in the mouth of the newborn pup, then give it to your Collie, who will take over. Most Rough Collies are wonderful mothers and it is very rare indeed that any problems will arise. Most bitches like to eat the placenta – it is nature's way of supplying protein. The only problem is that the placenta, when eaten, acts as a laxative and so it is advisable, if the bitch has a big litter, to take some away before she has time to eat them all.

Note the time taken between each pup being born, this can be anything from five minutes to an hour. As each pup is born, weigh them and make a note of the colours or markings.

Some bitches whelp quickly and some take hours. In any case, do make sure the bitch is comfortable and not distressed in any way. If you are at all worried, do not hesitate to call the vet. If, after prolonged straining, nothing is happening and the bitch is becoming exhausted, it is most important to get help.

AFTER THE BIRTH

When your Collie has finished giving birth to her beautiful puppies, wash down her hindquarters with some warm water, making sure that you dry her thoroughly before putting her back with the puppies. While this is being done, run your eye over the pups to see if any defects are evident. Remove any abnormal pups before the bitch returns to the nest; she cannot count, but she will know if you take one away.

Now is the time to take all the soiled paper out of the box and replace with clean fleecy vet bedding, which you can obtain from most pet shops. It is crucial at this point to make sure that the puppies are warm and dry, and that the whelping box is in a draught-free place. If possible, put a heat pad under the bedding for extra warmth and comfort.

In a maiden bitch sometimes the milk does not come in straight away. Do not worry, as the puppies will have had the colostrum, which is the first secretion from the mammary glands that occurs after giving birth. It is important that the puppies get this colostrum as it gives them immunity until

Even after the pups start weaning, they will continue to suckle for a time.

they are old enough to be vaccinated. This is why it is so important to make sure that your Collie is vaccinated before she is mated.

THE NURSING MOTHER

Most bitches will refuse to leave the newborn pups and I never make my bitches go out unless they really want to. Make sure no other dogs and visitors disturb the new mother, as this can affect the milk.

It is now essential that she has a good intake of calcium with vitamin D. Ask your vet for details of the correct dosage.

Light, nourishing meals (four a day) are needed for the first few days. Never give heavy meals just after whelping. Feed boiled chicken and rice or brown bread. Rough Collies also like scrambled eggs, but do not worry too much if she does not eat for the first day as she will be so busy with her puppies. Give her plenty of fresh milk if she will take it.

The first few days after whelping are vital to both pups and dam. You must check every few hours to see if all is well, that the pups are all drinking.

If you have a large litter, it would help your bitch if you could supplement some of the pups with a good-quality milk powder such as lactol, or you can ask your vet's advice.

The pups should gradually be weaned on to solid foods.

WEANING

At around ten to twelve days the fun begins, and it is time for you to introduce some solid food to the puppies. I grind up some good-quality beef, such as braising steak, and by putting some on the end of my finger, the pups soon suck it off. I do this three times a day, as well as letting them drink all they want from the mother.

By the time they are three weeks old they are having at least a dessertspoonful of raw meat three times a day, and at four weeks I introduce a soft cereal mixed with the meat. This way you will never have loose puppy stools.

From about five weeks old the pups will have the following diet, as well as a quick suckle from mum.

Breakfast

Any milky cereal such as porridge or baby rice.

Lunch

Raw, minced meat mixed with well-soaked biscuit or mixer.

Tea

As above, or scrambled eggs and brown bread.

Supper

Milky cereal.

Or you may wish to change over to a good all-in-one food. Do read the label and feeding guide.

As the pups continue to grow, I then introduce minced tripe with well-soaked puppy biscuit or mixer, or you may wish to use any of the good-quality, all-in-one foods that are so readily available.

You can worm your puppies from two weeks old if you are worried that they are not doing well or not putting on weight, but do ask for your vet's advice.

The best age for a puppy to go to its new home is at around eight weeks of age. By then they are not too dependant on littermates and will soon settle into a new home.

When an older pup leaves the nest, say at 12 or 14 weeks, it is much harder for the pup to adapt and he will quite often go off his food for a few days. This is because he does not have anyone to compete with and is confused when offered a whole bowl of food to himself. But most Collies are good eaters and most soon settle into a new family very well.

By eight weeks of age, a puppy is ready to go to his new home.

7 *The Rough Collie's Health*

The Rough Collie is a very healthy dog and is not prone to illnesses, but care must be taken to keep a watchful eye on your Collie's eating habits and daily routine. One of the first signs of a Collie being unwell is lack of appetite but, having said that, I must confess to have a bitch that will eat even if she is ill! Do find a good vet and build up a trusting relationship. You never know when you may need him.

THE MEDICINE CHEST

It is always a good idea to have a small cupboard in which to keep animal medicines safe, away from children and young animals. Once a year clear out all unused medicines and replace with fresh ones. You will need:

- Cotton wool or cotton pads.
- Scissors.
- Thermometer.
- Infra red lamp or electric heat pad.
- Eye dropper.
- Hypodermic syringes (5ml and 10ml), obtainable from your vet. These are very useful for administering liquid medicine.
- Nail clippers.
- Tweezers.
- Bandages.
- Milk of magnesia.
- Kaolin Poultice
- Saline solution or sterilised water.
- Olive oil.
- Ear cleaner.
- Vaseline.
- Worming tablets.
- Calcium with vitamin D.

ADMINISTERING MEDICINE

When giving medicine, always read the label very carefully before you administer the dose. If the dog cooperates, you may measure it out with a spoon but, if he is

not being helpful, then use one of your syringes. Insert the end in the side of the mouth and gently release the medicine.

To give tablets, open the dog's mouth, using finger and thumb on either side of the jaw. Open wide and place the pill as far back into the dog's throat as possible, pushing the tablet down the throat. Then close the dog's mouth and hold for a few seconds. Stroke the underside of the throat, as this will help the dog to swallow the tablet.

TREATING MINOR AILMENTS

This advice is for minor ailments only. At any time when you are not sure of what is wrong with your Collie, it is always advisable to phone your vet.

Cuts and abrasions: First cleanse the wound with mild antiseptic. You may use TCP or diluted Dettol. Check to see if more treatment is needed, or if it needs to be lightly bandaged.

Allergies: Some dogs, like humans, react to stings and pollen, and it is advisable to keep some Piriton syrup for such times. You may notice lumps under the skin and around the eyes and sometimes all over the body. Quite often this is caused by a change of diet, or the dog may have gone among nettles. If your Collie has any difficulty in breathing, you must seek medical advice, where an antihistamine injection will soon put things right.

WHEN TO CALL YOUR VET

The time to call your vet is when you have an emergency. If your Collie has had an accident, or is suddenly taken ill, never be afraid to call your vet, even in the middle of the night – that is what vets are for. But, if you do call in the night, make sure it really is an emergency. Have a pen and paper ready as, quite often, you will be given a locum vet number to call. Speak clearly, giving your name, telephone number and the symptoms of the dog.

WHAT IS AN EMERGENCY?

There are certain diseases or accidents that require emergency treatment.

BLOAT: Rough Collies rarely get bloat, but if your dog is in great pain and the stomach is full of gas, you must contact your vet immediately. No time must be lost. If your Collie suffers from digestive problems like this, then it is advisable to feed two small meals a day instead of one big one. Never allow your dog to

drink masses of water with his food and never allow exercise after feeding.

EYE INJURY: First apply a wet cloth over the injury and then head for the vet's surgery. It is important that you stop the dog from rubbing the injury.

POISONING: If you suspect your Collie has been poisoned, if at all possible take any evidence relating to the cause of poisoning with you. It will help the vet to determine the treatment.

DOG FIGHTS: If your Collie should become involved in a fight, although this will be very rare as Collies are not aggressive unless continually provoked, clean up the area surrounding the wound, unless there is a large, gaping wound or heavy loss of blood. Sometimes wounds look worse than they really are. By cleaning up, you can determine the extent of the damage, and whether a vet's attention is required.

ANAL GLANDS

Rough Collies are not prone to anal gland disease but, due to lack of a good diet, this may sometimes occur. The glands are situated either side of the anus. Normally the glands empty when the dog evacuates its bowels, but if you see your Collie trying to lick around its anus, or drag his or her bottom on the ground, just check the glands. If blocked glands are left unattended, an abscess could soon form. It is quite easy to empty the dog's anal glands but not a pleasant task for the faint-hearted. If your Collie has plenty of roughage in his diet, you should never have this problem.

ARTIFICIAL RESPIRATION

This is something important to learn as you never know when help may be needed. If, for any

reason, a Collie stops breathing, place the dog on a table lying on its side with the head hanging down over the edge. Pull the tongue out of the mouth and forward, placing your hand over the ribs and behind the shoulder blade to compress the chest. Expel the air in the lungs, release the pressure and allow the chest to expand and fill with air. Compress the chest about twelve times within one minute. At this stage check the gums for colour. The dog will gasp and try to sit up. Try to keep your Collie quiet and call the vet. You can also try mouth to nose resuscitation. Close the Collie's mouth and blow very gently up the nose until the Collie starts to gasp and breathe. If breathing starts, put a little brandy on the back of the tongue.

ASTHMA

Yes, even dogs can be asthmatic and the treatment is the same as for humans – a course of corticosteroids.

BAD BREATH

This can be caused by more than one factor. First check the teeth as sometimes an accumulation of tartar or tooth decay may be the culprit. If the smell persists, talk to

your vet, as it could be a sign of kidney malfunction.

BLINDNESS

Collies live to a very old age and, in some instances, may go blind. Collies have such an acute sense of hearing that this compensates to some extent. Providing you do not change your furniture around or put obstacles in the way, a blind dog will find its way around with no problems. Do take care never to let a Collie that is blind out on its own.

BURNS

If your Collie should be scalded, speed is of the utmost importance and, if possible, immerse your Collie in cold water to prevent further burning. Get to the vet immediately.

COLLIE NOSE

You will probably have heard of this though it is something we do not see much of these days. It can be caused by bright sunlight in the summer and bright snow in the winter months. The skin on the nose becomes crusted and very sore. Also, it may leave scars that are difficult to hide, as quite often the skin turns pink. If your Collie has a suspect allergy to the ultra violet rays of the sun, then do be sure to put a strong barrier cream all over the nose area.

CONSTIPATION

Unless your Collie is ill – and if this is the case, speak to your vet – the safest product to use is a little liquid paraffin added to the dinner. It is tasteless and has no smell, so it will not be detected. Plenty of roughage in the diet and a supply of fresh drinking water are musts.

DIARRHOEA

For non-specific diarrhoea, starve your Collie for twenty-four hours and give little water at frequent intervals. After fasting, give a very bland diet for a few days, such as cooked fish (no bones), lightly boiled chicken and rice. If the diarrhoea persists, contact your vet.

ENTERITIS

This is more serious than ordinary diarrhoea as it entails inflammation of the bowel, loss of appetite and vomiting, followed by excessive thirst. This can be brought on by a chill, or by swallowing some decomposed food that has been stolen, or even swallowing a foreign object such as a child's toy. Your vet will prescribe antibiotics, and warmth and rest will be the order of the day. Do not feed, but make sure the dog has plenty of fluids, and these must be offered little and often. Feed a very bland diet for a few days until the dog is fully recovered.

LOSS OF HAIR

If bald patches appear in your Collie's coat, it is advisable to get a skin scraping done to find out the reason. It may be a change of diet, change of carpet or even a different shampoo.

THE FEMALE CYCLE

If you have chosen a female then you must be aware that she will come into season once a year or, in some cases, every six or seven months. The first season normally occurs at about six to nine months of age. No Collie should be mated at this early age. The ideal time for a bitch to have a first litter, if this is what you intend, is at about eighteen months of age.

Most bitches will be in season for about three weeks. The first week the bitch will bleed quite heavily. This will continue into the second week when the vulva will swell and the colour of the discharge will change from blood red to a pale, straw colour. It will be at the end of the second week

and the beginning of the third week that your Collie will be most receptive to mating and will not be fussy as to the colour, shape or breed of male that comes to call.

If you do not want to breed from your Collie, I suggest you have her spayed, but do wait until she has had at least one season, to make sure she is fully developed. The right time to have your bitch spayed is either two months after she has been in season, or midway between seasons.

PYOMETRA

Sometimes an older bitch that has not been spayed can get an infection of the womb. This is called pyometra and usually happens after a prolonged season.

Symptoms are a smelly discharge from the vulva plus excessive drinking, and some bitches become unsteady as they walk. Sometimes she just seems to be off-colour, inclined to run a temperature, and have none of her normal zest. This must be attended to, as the condition can prove fatal if not checked. You must seek medical advice because she will need a hysterectomy. I had a bitch of 13 years old who came through the operation with no trouble and lived to be almost 15 years old.

FALSE PREGNANCY

Some bitches are prone to false pregnancies, sometimes called phantom pregnancies. This is not due to over-maternal feelings but the result of hormone imbalance. Some Collies even come into full lactation when this happens. Often, then, it is advisable to have her spayed.

MASTITIS

Some Collie bitches are prone to mastitis. This is an inflammation of the mammary glands which can occur during and after pregnancy. It can be most painful, and sometimes, an abscess may form. An early symptom to watch for is hardening around the teat area. If

the bitch is nursing, you will find that the puppies will not suckle from these teats.

The condition occurs when the bitch has a build-up of milk. A very maternal bitch will come into milk before the puppies are born, but mastitis can also happen when there is a small litter, or if the pups are too weak to suckle, which causes the teats to go hard and lumpy. The vet will prescribe antibiotics, but you can help by placing warm flannels over the sore area and expressing some of the milk. The antibiotics will not harm any suckling puppies.

THE MALE COLLIE

The male does not have any of these problems, but it is wise to examine the sheath of the Collie's penis as, sometimes, this can become dirty and infection can get under the skin. If you see your Collie licking himself in that area, take a quick look to see if all is well. Sometimes a hair may irritate, so it is wise to check once a week.

CASTRATION

Having your Collie castrated is a choice you have to make for yourself. If you do not want to breed from your male, then it is an option open to you, as castration

will prevent your Collie from straying. It will not alter his character. He will still be loyal and loving. However, care must be taken with diet, as the castrated male does tend to put on weight and, if you are not careful, you will end up with a fat Collie. Do remember that once your male Collie has been used at stud he will always be on the lookout for another bitch to mate. Unless your Rough Collie is a top show winner it is unfair to allow him to be used at stud.

HEREDITARY DISEASES

Here the Rough Collie is lucky as, although there have been a few Collies with hip dysplasia, the breed is not rife with this dreadful, painful condition. Also, the Rough Collie has a huge gene pool to work with and, should a problem arise, it is quite easy to eradicate it in a few generations.

The breed is not so lucky with the eyes, though, as most Collie breeds suffer with the recessive gene for Collie Eye Anomaly (CEA). This is an ocular defect, which is present at birth, with one or more distinct and sometimes unrelated features appearing in affected eyes. Although CEA can be severe and, sometimes, cause blindness, the defects are often so slight that both dog and owner are unaware of the problem.

Most breeders are very careful with their breeding stock and will only embark on a breeding programme with eye-tested stock. When you are buying your puppy, or choosing a stud dog, or buying a brood bitch, check to ensure that it has been eye-tested and certified clear by a qualified eye specialist. Mild CEA does not affect the Collie in its normal daily life and, even if a Collie has CEA more severely, it will still be able to lead a useful life as a companion. It is most rare that a Collie will go blind from this defect unless it has a detached retina.

PARASITES

Endoparasites live within the body and there are a number of types which affect dogs.

Roundworm (*Toxocara Canis*): This parasite is long, thin and pointed at both ends. The roundworm larvae lie dormant in the bitch, but when she becomes pregnant the larvae will migrate to the uterus and into the unborn puppies and that is why all puppies have roundworm.

If you are going to mate your bitch, make sure that she has been wormed prior to the mating. Bitches who have not been wormed will produce puppies that, by the time they are a few weeks old, will be full of worms. They will have diarrhoea, poor, harsh coats, hard, distended stomachs and they will cry, making a mewing sound.

There is a safe wormer which you can obtain from your vet that can be used from day two of birth, and if it is used as directed, you should have no problems. If left untreated, these worms can cause untold damage in young stock and can lead to death.

Tapeworm: If you keep your Collie clean and free from fleas, you should never see a tapeworm. It is the common flea that acts as the intermediate host. A Collie that is infested with tapeworm will soon lose condition.

Tapeworms are easy to identify as the segments will appear in the dog's stools. The worm itself is made up of two distinct sections: the head and the segmented body. The segments break up and appear in the dog's stools, looking very much like flat rice. Sometimes these rice-like segments stick to the dog's coat on the underside of the tail and around the anus.

The tapeworm can sometimes

be as long as eighteen or more inches (45 cms). If left untreated, it can break up. The dog then passes the rice-like segments but retains the head, which is smaller than a pinhead. This then attaches itself to the intestinal wall, causing much discomfort. Sometimes a dog may drag his bottom along the ground.

Fleas spread tapeworm, and there are several stages. The flea sucks the dog's blood, then lays its eggs in the dog's bedding or in the carpets and soft furnishings. If your Collie ingested the flea while biting itself, the wormheads are then released into the dog's intestine and mature into adult tapeworms. The eggs that were in the bedding and carpets hatch into larvae. They feed on dust and soon the larvae form a cocoon. In less than fifteen days the flea emerges, to start all over again.

One flea can lay over 500 eggs

in a lifetime, and the tapeworm can produce thousands of eggs in each tiny segment. The flea feeds off these eggs, starting the procedure once more. This sounds dreadful – but both fleas and tapeworms are quite simple to destroy. Follow a routine of worming your dog on a regular basis and use a good flea spray in your home, paying extra attention to the dog's sleeping area. It is advisable to use a total worming product. Flea collars are very good, but they are not ideal on a Rough Collie, as they interfere with the huge neck coat. A good flea spray should suffice.

Heartworm: This is not often diagnosed in the UK, but it is prevalent in other countries, including the USA. When a dog is imported into the UK from an area that has a problem, the dog would be on heartworm medication for a few months to

A healthy, happy Rough Collie makes a wonderful, loving companion.

make sure that it is clear of any infection. This type of worm is transmitted by the bite of an infected mosquito, and it can take up to six months for the worm to develop in the heart.

Hookworm: These leech-like parasites are not common in the UK, but are found elsewhere. They live on blood that is sucked from the intestinal walls. This causes anaemia, fits and a drastic loss of appetite in the dog.

HOMOEOPATHIC MEDICINE

There are many people today who are regular users of homoeopathic medicines but it should be remembered that they should only be used for common ailments.

- Aconite is often used for travel sickness.
- Apis Mel for insect bites.
- Argent Nit for colic and flatulence.
- Arnica for bruises and sprains.
- Arson B for loss of appetite.
- Belladonna for heat stroke.
- Calc Fluor for incontinence in older bitches.
- Carbo Veg for bad breath.
- Euphrasia for hayfever.
- Gelsimium for nervousness in show animals.
- Phosphorus for anxiety caused by the sudden noise of fireworks or thunder.
- Sulphur for offensive smells.
- Thuja for warty growths.

Before using any of these medicines, speak to a person who specialises in homoeopathic remedies and who is qualified to give advice.